Bourbon Assignments
Scored Things to Do in Bourbon for 2022

by

Colonel Steve Akley

Note: Get Colonel Steve to sign that line above and you get ten bonus points before you even get started!

Bourbon Assignments

Written by:
Colonel Steve Akley

Published by: ABV Network, LLC

Text copyright © 2021 Steve Akley

Cover illustration by Mark Hansen

ISBN - 978-0-9997585-1-9

Philosophy:

Written for bourbon fans, by a bourbon fan. *(That means something to me, I hope it does to you, too.)*

- Colonel Steve Akley

Dedication:

This book is dedicated to the great Freddie Johnson of Buffalo Trace. His job title is tour guide, but he means so much more to all of us. I don't know a single person that has turned more people into lifelong bourbon fans than Freddie Johnson. If we could all look at the world like Freddie does, it would definitely be a better place. His resume reads Kentucky Bourbon Hall-of-Fame, but he's a hall-of-famer in life. Freddie, this book, designed to get bourbon fans involved in the spirit we both love, is dedicated to you and all you represent to bourbon fans everywhere!

Bourbon Assignments

Foreword by:
Bernie Lubbers

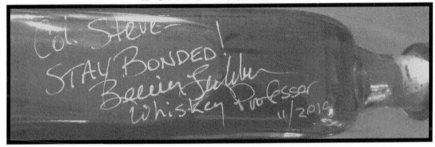

In my career as Whiskey Ambassador at Heaven Hill Distillery, I'm paid to travel all over the country and attend most bourbon and whiskey shows. (My home base is Louisville, Kentucky.) Time-after-time at whiskey shows around the country, and here around Louisville and Bardstown, Kentucky I kept seeing this one particular guy again-and-again. I asked a fellow whiskey ambassador I was with on such a sighting, "so who's the dude in the glasses?"

He said, "You don't know Steve Akley?"

… I do now.

You see I get paid to travel all over the country and attend these events, so when you see someone at these events on their own dime, it's impressive. After meeting Steve, I found out that he is not only a passionate fan, but a nice guy. Like good whiskey, the additional time in the bourbon barrel he has built a great reputation in the bourbon world and is gaining quite a following of other passionate folks. And not just through a podcast or YouTube Channel, but he's building a whole damn Network, and a fine reputation in the industry along the way.

I'm sure this will not be the last project that Steve writes on bourbon, and whatever that is, I'm sure that I will read it, and I'm glad you are reading it too. I look forward to what he creates next, and when he does, I will pour a nice Bottled In Bond whiskey while I read it.

So pour yourself a nice Bottled In Bond Whiskey, and read about your bourbon assignments awaiting you here in Kentucky, and don't be surprised if you see the "dude in the glasses," at one of the watering holes here in town.

Bernie Lubbers – The Whiskey Professor

Bernie Lubbers

Note: Get Bernie to sign that line above and you get another ten bonus points!

Bourbon Assignments

40 Things to do in the World of Bourbon for 2022

Introduction by:
Colonel Steve Akley, Author

The idea for this book really invented itself. So many people ask me what are some cool things to do when you travel to Kentucky, or what they should be doing while they are there. People also ask me what I do when I'm in Kentucky. I do spend a lot of time there, so I thought it would be a good idea to curate a list of everything I enjoy doing. While none of these are things I do exclusively, of course, as a whole it represents "My Kentucky," the things I love to do when I am there.

Why would I do this?

Well, I truly appreciate so much of what the Bluegrass State has to offer when I am visiting. It's my home away from home and there are many things I do there that I miss when I'm at my real actual home in St. Louis. Many of these activities in this book are things I love doing again-and-again when I'm there.

I also wrote this book as we were still wrapped up in a battle against a global pandemic. Many of the businesses featured here have struggled recently as they have had to deal with fewer customers and attempts to pivot their businesses to cater to the world we suddenly find ourselves living in. With this in mind, the book is a bit of a love note to those businesses. We care and appreciate what they do for our lives and our happiness. Sure, we probably haven't visited as frequently recently, but it doesn't mean we don't care. We look forward to getting back to normal and seeing them on the regular again soon.

It's also a way of giving back. So many great things have happened to me since I've started working in the bourbon industry. Many of these places featured either directly contributed to the success I've experienced, or at a minimum provided me with a little joy when I'm away from home trying to get established in the world of bourbon. What better way to say "thank you" then to create a book that encourages people to visit, to interact with the business owners and employees and to spend some money while we are there?

This book is designed to be your travel companion on these trips. It's your invitation to visit all of the things I love. It's meant to be used for the next year, to help set your journey, log your adventures and create memories by having it signed by people you meet along the way.

Well, have fun living the Colonel Steve life in Kentucky. Who knows, maybe you will bump into me on one of your stops?

After all, these are my favorite places!

Table of Contents

How Does This Work?

The biggest question that has to be is how does this work?

After all, there are assignments, and scores, so what does this mean?

Well, don't worry, it's actually pretty simple. This book is as much of a workbook as it is a travel guide. I envision copies of this book to be beat up, dog-eared and written all over by the end of 2022 if you are doing this correctly. The book itself is a pretty comprehensive look at the things I love to do in bourbon... most of which occurs in Kentucky. Each "assignment" has a point value of 1, 5 or 10 points assigned to it. Additionally, there are other ways to get bonus points while you are there. It may be buying a certain item that is my favorite on the menu if it's a restaurant or an activity I think you need to complete at a distillery. Remember, this book is my answer to what you should do in Kentucky, I'm getting as specific as I can here.

Each chapter, or assignment as it is presented, has a mini worksheet allowing you to give your score for that particular section. This book is designed to have you getting out, visiting and accumulating points for your assignments any time between your purchase of the book and December 31, 2022. You can then submit your grand total for all of your scores to me via email by midnight on December 31, 2022. Instructions and a place to tally all of your scores are in the Grand Total Worksheet at the end of the book.

There is a prize involved, but it has no cash value. It's more along the lines of sharing your experiences with your bourbon travels and assignments with our audience on my podcast, The Bourbon Daily. This top-ranked show has a large audience of enthused bourbon fans who would love to hear about what you did in the world of bourbon.

With this in mind, the top ten scores will be invited to appear on an episode with me and the team to talk some bourbon with you (if we have some ties, we may take one or two extra, but if there are many tied for the top ten, we'll break the tie via a random drawing). I look forward to being able to hear your stories of visiting these places and what you had fun doing.

Here's to the adventures this book brings you.

Cheers!

1 Pointers

A Special Drink on Whiskey Row

The Bar at Fort Nelson

Inside the Bar at Fort Nelson (Photo: Michter's)

Address: 801 W Main St, Louisville, KY 40202
Website: michters.com/thebar

Michter's owns the ultimate distillery bourbon bar. It's as close to fact as you can get with such a subjective topic, but I feel very safe stating that. First off, it looks like it was taken from the set of the Mad Men TV show. It's all swanky 60s brought back to life that has you looking for Don Draper sitting in the corner drinking an Old Fashioned. It's not just about the décor, though, it's the vibe, the knowledgeable and friendly staff and the great drink menu.

Scorecard for This Assignment:
Visit the Bar at Fort Nelson (1 Point): _____

Potential Bonus Points (Bonus Point(s) in Parenthesis):

Make it an Old Fashioned (1 Point): _____

TOTAL (2 Points Possible): _____

<u>Assignment #2</u>   Eat Your Bourbon

Shop Bourbon Foods/Ingredients

Bourbon Barrel Foods

Inside a Bourbon Barrel Foods shop (Photo: BBF)

Address: 1201 Story Avenue, Louisville, KY 40206
Website: bourbonbarrelfoods.com

Matt Jamie, owner of Bourbon Barrel Foods has something special in his brand. It's literally in the running for the best brand in bourbon that isn't actually bourbon. Whether it's a stand-alone product to enjoy by itself, an ingredient to make something or a condiment to enhance a different product, Bourbon Barrel Foods delivers offerings which are always of high quality and pack flavor. While you can find these products at places like distilleries, grocery stores and even liquor stores, it's worth the trip to go to one of their company stores so you can shop the entire lineup. You really haven't experienced

BOURBON ASSIGNMENTS | STEVE AKLEY, AUTHOR

Bourbon Barrel Foods unless you've tried their signature item, their Bluegrass Soy Sauce, the only soy sauce fermented and aged in bourbon barrels.

Scorecard for This Assignment:
Shop Bourbon Barrel Foods (1 Point): _____

Potential Bonus Points (Bonus Point(s) in Parenthesis):

Buy Bluegrass Soy Sauce (1 Point): _____

TOTAL (2 Points Possible): _____

Whiskey Row Dining Spot

Merle's Whiskey Kitchen

Outside of Merle's (Photo: Merle's)

Address: 122 W Main Street, Louisville, KY 40202
Website: merleswhiskeykitchen.com

There are so many places to go on Whiskey Row that you'll end up spending so much time there you need a place to dine. There are plenty of options, but why not go for the best in the area? The answer is Merle's Whiskey Kitchen. It's the perfect balance of amazing food, an excellent bourbon selection and live entertainment. Everything's good on the menu, but you have to get a side of their mac and cheese!

BOURBON ASSIGNMENTS | STEVE AKLEY, AUTHOR

Scorecard for This Assignment:
Dine at Merle's Whiskey Kitchen (1 Point): _____

Potential Bonus Points (Bonus Point(s) in Parenthesis):

Order the Lip Smack'n Mac & Cheese (1 Point): _____

TOTAL (2 Points Possible): _____

Assignment #4   100,000 Gallon Bottle

Bourbon Photo Op Time

The Old Forester Water Tower

It's one of a kind! (Photo: Brown-Forman)

Address: 850 Dixie Highway, Louisville, KY 40210
Website: brown-forman.com

Old Forester's iconic bourbon bottle water tower was constructed in 1936 at a cost of $100,000 (their entire advertising budget for the year). At over 60 feet tall, 20 feet in diameter and towering 218 feet off the ground, it has a capacity of 100,000 gallons, or over 50,000 750ml bottles. It's worth a drive by as you go through town, but if you can stop, a picture of you and 100,000 gallon bottle of OldFo is definitely worthy for the 'gram.

BOURBON ASSIGNMENTS | STEVE AKLEY, AUTHOR

Scorecard for This Assignment:

Drive by and see the tower (1 Point): _____

Potential Bonus Points (Bonus Point(s) in Parenthesis):

Get a photo with the tower in the background (1 Point): _____

TOTAL (2 Points Possible): _____

Assignment #5   It's a Beam Thing

Visit the Biggest Bourbon Brand

Jim Beam Distillery

Outside the Visitor's Center (Photo: Jim Beam)

Address: 568 Happy Hollow Rd, Clermont, KY 40110
Website: jimbeam.com

There are some that shun the Beam tour just because it's such a big brand. Surely, the biggest brand in the world can't give a tour that feels as intimate as a craft distiller, right? Well, you may be right there, but it's a totally different scale and level and while I love craft tours, you have to experience Beam just to see the size-and-scope of what they do. The tours is a thorough one that touches on brand history, the people of Beam, the products and production. They have a huge portfolio and you get to choose what you taste at the end. There are many iconic moments within a visit as well. You can stand alongside Jim Beam himself via his statue in front of the distillery. You can pay your respects to Booker and his beloved dog Dot with his statue on the grounds. Of course, whether you need a break or not, you simply must sit on those rockers in front of the visitors center. It has an Anytown, USA, feel to it and it's a great place to people watch.

Scorecard for This Assignment:
Take a Beam Tour (1 Point): _____

Potential Bonus Points (Bonus Point(s) in Parenthesis):

Get a photo with the Jim Beam Statue (1 Point): _____

Pay respects at the Booker Noe statue (1 Point): _____

Sit on a rocking chair on the porch (1Point): _____

TOTAL (4 Points Possible): _____

Assignment #6   Coffee & Bourbon

Bourbon Celebrity Hangout

Fante's Coffee Shop

That famous roaster (Photo: Fante's Coffee Shop)

Address: 2501 Grinstead Drive, Louisville, KY 40206
Website: fantescoffee.com

A planned "random" bourbon celebrity sighting can be a challenge if you aren't at their place of business. If you wander into Fante's Coffee, though, you never know who you might spot from the world of bourbon. Owner Leo Fante's brother Stephen, who is the well-known brand ambassador/single barrel curator for Limestone Branch stops in almost every day to get a cup of java. I've seen Bernie Lubbers and Jackie Zykan there. Our team from the ABV Network always stops by when they are in town. Even if you don't catch someone who is "bourbon famous" there, their roaster is pretty famous itself. It looks like it belongs in a distillery near the still. Come see why such big brands as Limestone Branch and Michter's trust Fante's Coffee to make their house brands. You can even get a bourbon... now that's pure Kentucky!

BOURBON ASSIGNMENTS | STEVE AKLEY, AUTHOR

Scorecard for This Assignment:

Get a cup at Fante's (1 Point): _____

Potential Bonus Points (Bonus Point(s) in Parenthesis):

Buy a custom roasted bag (1 Point): _____

TOTAL (2 Points Possible): _____

<u>Assignment #7</u>   <u>Legendary Status</u>

Drink Where They Drank

The Old Seelbach Bar

Inside the bar (Photo: Hilton)

Address: 500 S 4th St, Louisville, KY 40202
Website: seelbachhilton.com

The Old Seelbach Hotel (now part of the Hilton family), serves as one of the backdrops of F. Scott Fitzgerald's the Great Gatsby. Supposedly, Fitzgerald, a frequent guest of the hotel bar, met George Remus who served as the inspiration for the character of Jay Gatsby. You can't help but feel the history in the place as you enjoy a drink even if the bar isn't in the same place in the hotel when Fitzgerald and Remus where there. The bar staff can point you to the basement, and its unbelievable architecture where you can see where the Old Rathskeller Bar was and those famous meetings. Al Capone was also a frequent guest at the hotel as well. Famously, he used to love to run card games there. If you are lucky and get the right staff member, and no one has rented the room, you might be able to talk your way into a tour of the Capone Room.

Scorecard for This Assignment:
Drink at The Old Seelbach Bar (1 Point): _____

Potential Bonus Points (Bonus Point(s) in Parenthesis):

Order a Seelbach Cocktail (1 Point): _____

Visit the basement Cocktail (1 Point): _____

TOTAL (3 Points Possible): _____

<u>Assignment #8</u>   Photo Ops Galore

Pose with Colonel Sanders

Louisville Visitor's Center

The Colonel (Photo: Louisville Visitor's Center)

Address: 301 S. 4th Street (Jefferson Street), Louisville, KY 40202
Website: gotolouisville.com

With the emergence of the internet, most visitor's centers are an antiquated concept. Louisville has kept its relevant by making it a fun stop loaded with Kentucky and bourbon souvenirs and a couple of really great photo opportunities. On the way in, you will see the famous Louisville pronunciation sign. Is it Looeyville, Looaville, Luhvul or other possibilities? I'm not sure even a lifetime Louisvillian has that one figured out. It does make a fun social media post, though. The real treasure here, though, is a life-size Colonel Sander mannequin, complete with the signature white suit, string tie, cane and bucket of chicken. Be sure to say, "secret recipe" on three to get that perfect smile when taking that photo.

Scorecard for This Assignment:
Stop by the Louisville Visitor's Center (1 Point): _____

Potential Bonus Points (Bonus Point(s) in Parenthesis):

Get a photo with Col. Sanders (1 Point): _____

Post the Louisville pronunciation sign (1 Point): _____

TOTAL (3 Points Possible): _____

Get a Tinfoil Sandwich

Handy Food Mart

Homemade gloriousness! (Photo: Col. Steve)

Address: 3945 New Sheperdsville Road, Bardstown, KY 40004
Website: handyfoodmartky.com

Tinfoil breakfast sandwiches are one of the hardest things to explain that makes Kentucky so unique. I mean every fast food place and many gas stations across the country feature breakfast sandwiches. Most have some sort of foil paper they wrap them in, but the tinfoil sandwiches in Kentucky are unique. Why you are probably asking? Well, they are actual homemade sandwiches, not pre-assembled and then microwaved like you find at gas stations outside of Kentucky. What's also so great is they are literally everywhere. If you walk into a random gas station, there is a pretty good chance they are going to be cooking up sandwiches and wrapping them in tinfoil. Now, I've listed the Handy Food Mart here because it's one I always hit on my way into Bardstown. Half of the fun of this assignment is finding your own, though as you explore Kentucky during your bourbon travels.

Scorecard for This Assignment:
Breakfast at the Handy Food Mart/Bardstown (1 Point): _____

Potential Bonus Points (Bonus Point(s) in Parenthesis):

Get it like Steve does/Hot Jake Sausage (1 Point): _____

Make it a true KY breakfast with an Ale-8-One (1 Point): _____

Discover your own Tinfoil Sandwich place (1 Point): _____

TOTAL (4 Points Possible): _____

Assignment #10   Bourbon Shoppin'

Can a Liquor Store be Legendary?

Toddy's Liquors

Toddy's (Photo: Steve Akley)

Address: 110 South 4th St, Bardstown, KY 40004
Website: facebook.com/toddysliquors

Are there better prices and bigger selections in bourbon? Absolutely, but there's only one Toddy's. Toddy Beam (yes, those Beams) opened Toddy's Liquors in 1960. This Bardstown institution is on the must visit list, even if you can't explain exactly why.

The crowded, claustrophobia-inducing layout, those bowed wooden shelves and owner Gutherie McKay who has held court there for over 35-years after buying out Toddy Beam make up a unique experience that makes you feel like you are going back in time to a different era in bourbon. Sure, the conversation might be how much things suck in bourbon right now, or why something is so expensive, but I'm telling you that even if you aren't feeling it while you are there, you'll be oddly pulled back to going again the next time you are in town. This place is just that special.

Scorecard for This Assignment:

Visit Toddy's Liquors (1 Point): _____

Potential Bonus Points (Bonus Point(s) in Parenthesis):

Buy a barrel pick (1 Point): _____

TOTAL (2 Points Possible): _____

Assignment #11   Shop for Unicorns

Score Big at the HH Gift Shop!

Heaven Hill Bourbon Heritage Center

Lined up and waiting (Photo: Steve Akley)

Address: 1311 Gilkey Run Rd, Bardstown, KY 40004
Website: heavenhilldistillery.com

I once was one of those people that swore I would never stand in line for bourbon. I mean I love bourbon, particularly those things that are hard to find. There is something oddly satisfying with a real sense of accomplishment about scoring a coveted bottle, even if it's nothing more than dumb luck.

Even with that in mind, I always thought my time was too valuable to bother actually just waiting around to score a bottle. Boy, was I wrong. When my buddy Jeremy Schell convinced me to spend a night at Four Roses to score a bottle of Al Young, I instantly became hooked. The stories that are shared, the camaraderie you gain with your fellow bourbon fans and that sense of accomplishment, not for just stumbling into a random bottle but "earning" it by those hours in line made it so unique and wonderful.

You don't have to spend the night to feel what it's like to score some bourbon. You can simply lineup at Heaven Hill about an hour before they open. Each day they typically release something cool like an Old Fitzgerald decanter or a Parker's Heritage. Even if you don't snag a unicorn, you get some great time with other bourbon fans and you can always buy one of those Elijah Craig "grenades," which is like the official consolation prize of the bourbon world.

Scorecard for This Assignment:
Line up at the Heaven Hill Gift Shop (1 Point): _____

Potential Bonus Points (Bonus Point(s) in Parenthesis):

Score a Cool Bottle (1 Point): _____

Add a Grenade (1 Point): _____

TOTAL (3 Points Possible): _____

<u>Assignment #12   It Gets A Little Crazy</u>

Pair Your Bourbon with Art

Proof on Main

Just look for David! (Photo: Proof on Main)

Address: 702 W Main St, Louisville, KY 40202
Website: proofonmain.com

A recent check of Proof on Main's spirits menu yielded over 30 different barrel picks to choose from. This sort of commitment means it has to make your "to do" list of places to go.

While the bourbon selection is amazing, the food doesn't disappoint. The menu offers a wide array of types and styles of food and while I don't have the most adventurous palate, I'm comfortable endorsing anything on the menu based on the friends' reviews I've dined with there.

My highest recommendation goes to their Bison Burger. I mean come on... a burger that low in fat... it's damn near eating healthy making it my go-to at Proof.

BOURBON ASSIGNMENTS | STEVE AKLEY, AUTHOR

Of course, if you just dine at Proof you are missing something seriously cool… a stroll through the art gallery at their sister hotel the 21c. It's eclectic, interactive and just plain fun. Guys, you have to stop by the men's room in the hotel where a one-way mirrored wall allows you to look out into the hotel while you are in the restroom. It's kinda freaky!

Scorecard for This Assignment:
Dine at Proof on Main (1 Point): _____

Potential Bonus Points (Bonus Point(s) in Parenthesis):

Get the Bison Burger (1 Point): _____

Order a Barrel Pick (1 Point): _____

Stroll Through 21c's Art Installation (1 Point): _____

TOTAL (4 Points Possible): _____

Assignment #13   Visit DSP-KY-5

History Brought Back to Life

James E. Pepper Distillery

Old DSP-KY-5 (Photo: James E. Pepper Distillery)

Address: 1228 Manchester Street, UNIT 100, Lexington, KY 40504
Website: jamesepepper.com

James E. Pepper Distillery owner did something that seems so overwhelming to me that I can't even begin to fathom how he did it. He managed to not only bring back a historic brand, he also salvaged its old decaying headquarters and it's turned in to this amazing place to visit. The Distillery District of Lexington, once the home to the James E. Pepper campus, now houses multiple distilleries, bars, restaurants and other cool businesses. It's one-stop entertainment venue where you can spend an entire day hanging out and exploring.

BOURBON ASSIGNMENTS | STEVE AKLEY, AUTHOR

The tour itself is great. You get to try some new make as well as their product lineup. They often have special bottles available only through the gift shop. It's a great visit to not only see a cool production distillery, but to learn about the history of this brand. Amir Peay has done an excellent job of curating a lot of historical artifacts from this business and you really start to see how important this brand was.

After your tour, head right next door to Goodfella's Pizza to grab a slice so you've got plenty of energy to hit the rest of the places in the Distillery District. Save room for dessert, though, because Crank & Boom's next on our list!

Scorecard for This Assignment:
Take a tour at James E. Pepper (1 Point): _____

Potential Bonus Points (Bonus Point(s) in Parenthesis):

Buy a bottle in the gift shop (1 Point): _____

Stop at Goodfella's for a slice (1 Point): _____

TOTAL (3 Points Possible): _____

Bourbon + Ice Cream = Winning!

Crank & Boom Craft Ice Cream Makers

Crank & Boom (Photo: Steve Akley)

Address: 1210 Manchester St, Lexington, KY 40504
Website: crankandboom.com

Visiting distilleries can be exhausting. I mean there's a lot of walking on the tours, there's the drinking and don't forget the shopping at the gift shop. Sometimes you just gotta take a quick break and Crank & Boom offers you the perfect place to just relax for a few minutes enjoying some uber flavorful ice cream.

Situated right between James E. Pepper Distillery and Barrel House Distillery in Lexington's Distillery District, Crank and Boom has a menu that has a couple of different options that incorporate bourbon, Bourbon Ball and Bourbon & Honey. I've tried them both and can definitely give you my highest recommendation on those, but, I'm also kind of partial to their Gooey Butter Cake since that's a St. Louis original.

Scorecard for This Assignment:
Try at least one of the bourbon offerings (1 Point): _____

Potential Bonus Points (Bonus Point(s) in Parenthesis):

Get a second scoop of Gooey Butter Cake (1 Point): _____

TOTAL (2 Points Possible): _____

Assignment #15   Palace of the Palates

Get Your Kicks... w/Barrel Picks

Westport Whiskey and Wine

Great whiskey straight ahead (Photo: Steve Akley)

Address: 1115 Herr Ln #140, Louisville, KY 40222
Website: westportwhiskeyandwine.com

Barrel picks have really taken over the bourbon industry. Fans, perhaps tired of chasing allocated bourbon they can't find, have turned their attention to barrel picks, the single barrels of bourbon purchased by bars, restaurants, liquor stores and bourbon clubs. The goal with these picks is always to find something off-profile from the normal shelf offering.

Now, I can guarantee your barrel pick is probably going to be off-profile when you pick up a barrel pick but that's not necessarily always a good thing. You see, there are good barrel picks and there are bad barrel picks. What separates

Westport Whiskey and Wine from most picking barrels is their picks aren't just on the side of being "good barrel picks," they typically reside at the top of the heap. Mongo Excellent Good Barrel picks might be an accurate descriptor.

So, it's comforting to know that when you pick up one of their barrel picks you are probably onto something delightful. Still not convinced? No worries, they've got a tasting bar where you can actually try before you buy so you really don't have much to lose here. Stop by Westport Whiskey and Wine and find something special you can share with friends!

<u>Scorecard for This Assignment:</u>
Visit Westport Whiskey and Wine (1 Point): _____

Potential Bonus Points (Bonus Point(s) in Parenthesis):

Buy a Barrel Pick (1 Point): _____

Taste Something at the Tasting Bar (1 Point): _____

TOTAL (3 Points Possible): _____

Assignment #16   Chef Edward Lee

4th Street Live Dining

Whiskey Dry

Whiskey Dry (Photo: Whiskey Dry)

Address: 412 S 4th Street, Louisville, KY 40202
Website: whiskeydryrestaurant.com

There is a lot to like about Ed Lee. He's got some really creative takes on cuisine. He's incredibly generous with his time and his money. He really worked hard to make a difference during the pandemic to the restaurant industry. You might think a business owner with a burgeoning empire and civil mindedness like Ed Lee would be incredibly serious all the time. In reality, Chef Edward Lee is one of the most laid back and funny people you will ever meet.

What truly is the coolest thing about Ed Lee, though, is the fact he's one of us... yes, he's just a bourbon fan. So many people use bourbon as a way to make money and while they profess their love for everything bourbon, a quick conversation lets you know they are more fans of what bourbon gives them then they are the distilled spirit. With Ed Lee, he truly is a fan of bourbon, it's history, brands and people.

His restaurant, Whiskey Dry, is a highlight if you find yourself in the 4th Street Live area of downtown Louisville. Pre-covid, this covered street section of downtown was a hub of activity... live music, competitions, street performers, restaurants, bars, etc. I like Whiskey Dry because it's got a great bourbon selection, the burgers are excellent and that bourbon shake... yowza!

Scorecard for This Assignment:
Visit Whiskey Dry (1 Point): _____

Potential Bonus Points (Bonus Point(s) in Parenthesis):

Order a bourbon (1 Point): _____

Get the Big Ed Burger (1 Point): _____

Add the Bourbon Chocolate Shake (1 Point): _____

   TOTAL (4 Points Possible): _____

"I can only tour one distillery."

Old Forester Distillery Tour

Charring a barrel (Photo: Steve Akley)

Address: 119 W Main Street, Louisville, KY 40202
Website: oldforester.com

A question that I get asked a lot is, "I'm going to Louisville and I've only got time for one distillery tour, where should I go?"

BOURBON ASSIGNMENTS | STEVE AKLEY, AUTHOR

First of all, your trip planning is all wrong. If you only have time for one tour, you're doing something wrong. Make more time than that people!

Okay, that public service announcement aside, I guess if you are there for business and your time is really tight, if I had to limit myself to just one tour (which I wouldn't, but I'm trying to play the game here), I think Old Forester is the choice. I mean it's got a lot going for it.

First, it's the history. They are in the exact spot where the company started. Second, they do some cool releases in the gift shop. We're talking gift-shop-only offerings like President's Choice or allocated items like Birthday Bourbon.

I also like the fact you see the entire process of making whiskey from fermentation to distillation to ageation (okay, I made that last word up, but they do have an onsite rickhouse). Because Brown-Forman makes its own barrels, you even get to see how they do that in an onsite cooperage with the highlight being one of the tour guests getting to push the button to give a barrel a blast of fire to char it.

Oh yeah, there's a chance you might see Jackie Z there as well. Yeah, OldFo is definitely the pick if you can only go to one Louisville distillery.

Scorecard for This Assignment:
Take and OldFo Tour (1 Point): _____

Potential Bonus Points (Bonus Point(s) in Parenthesis):

Volunteer to Ignite the Barrel During a Tour (1 Point): _____

TOTAL (2 Points Possible): _____

Assignment #18 Casa de Brauner

The World's Best Bourbon Bar

Bourbons Bistro

I'm drawn to this sign like a moth to light (Photo: Steve Akley)

Address: 2255 Frankfort Avenue, Louisville, KY 40206
Website: bourbonsbistro.com

As soon as you walk inside Bourbons Bistro you feel like you are at the epicenter of bourbon. You've got Jason Brauner holding court behind the bar, superstar bartenders Mike and Emma serving up pours and a slew of bourbon celebrities sitting in those barstools. Seriously, just talk to the people at the bar and you will be amazed to find out what their job in bourbon is. I've met more industry people there through the years than anywhere else.

It's not just about the bourbon, either. The food is fantastic. I love the burger and the pork chop is other-worldly.

I'll walk in and I'll see bartender Mike Downs pull out the Wild Turkey 101 Rye and filling up a glass for me. That never gets old!

Plus, if you get the chance to talk to Jason, either at the bar, or even better out front at their bistro tables, you get to talk bourbon with one of the most respected people in bourbon. If he likes you, he may even invite you up to his office with his vast personal collection of whiskey where he'll likely share a pour or two with you.

It's the absolute best!

Scorecard for This Assignment:
Visit Bourbons Bistro (1 Point): _____

Potential Bonus Points (Bonus Point(s) in Parenthesis):

Order the pork chop for dinner (1 Point): _____

Enjoy a round sitting at the bistro tables in front (1 Point): _____

Ask Mike the bartender for Akley's regular pour (1 Point): _____

Score an invite to Jason's office (3 Points): _____

TOTAL (7 Points Possible): _____

Sometimes You Just Need A Steak

Jeff Ruby's Steakhouse

Inside Jeff Ruby's (Photo: Jeff Ruby's)

Address: 325 West Main Street, Louisville, KY 40202
Website: jeffruby.com

I'm pretty cheap, but every once-in-awhile you have to go all out. Jeff Ruby's is one of the special places where it feels good to splurge. After all, they do promote the fact you get the "Jeff Ruby Experience," when you are there which is basically a dedication to customer satisfaction. Jeff Ruby is a real person, and I can tell you he lives the idea of the Jeff Ruby Experience. His team goes all out to ensure your meal at his restaurant is special.

The food is top notch, the décor is cool, the place is impeccable in terms of cleanliness (Jeff would have it no other way) and they have a piano player there that is unbelievable. The last time I was there, the St. Louis Blues were making their run to the Stanley Cup and we kept tipping him to play the classic big band song, *St. Louis Blues* and the old 80s pop song *Gloria*, which was the team's adopted fight song that year. It was so cool. When we left, he even "played us out" as we filed out of the restaurant with one last play of *Gloria*.

Amazing!

I think it was truly a Jeff Ruby Experience.

Scorecard for This Assignment:
Dine at Jeff Ruby's Louisville (1 Point): _____

Potential Bonus Points (Bonus Point(s) in Parenthesis):

Start with the Tiger Shrimp Cocktail (1 Point): _____

Order the Blackened Ribeye (2 Points): _____

Get the Blue Cheese Cap for Your Steak (1 Point): _____

TOTAL (5 Points Possible): _____

Assignment #20   Events from Home

Let Us Bring Kentucky To You!

Virtual Bourbon Events

Freddie Noe of Jim Beam on an Event (Photo: Steve Akley)

Address: Your house!
Website: abvnetwork.com/virtual

While not much good has come out of a global pandemic, one thing that has turned out pretty well is virtual bourbon events. The technology of platforms like Zoom allow us to gather with friends even when you couldn't do that at our favorite establishments. It also taught us you can do some pretty cool types of events without having to worry about driving, finding a spot to park or even getting out of your sweat pants.

The ABV Network established itself as the leader in at-home bourbon events via its Virtual Bourbon division established in 2020. Topics include blind tastings, events hosted by bourbon celebrities and the tasting of old, aka "dusty" bourbon. Some of the best conversations happen after the official event ends and we turn off the recording and just chat with friends.

Join us for one, or maybe a dozen of these events!

Scorecard for This Assignment:
Attend a Virtual Bourbon Event (1 Point): _____

Potential Bonus Points (Bonus Point(s) in Parenthesis):

Hangout with the Group After it Ends (1 Point): _____

TOTAL (2 Points Possible): _____

<u>Assignment #21</u>   <u>A Flavor Explosion</u>

Get a Peerless Gift Shop Pick

Kentucky Peerless Distilling Co.

There they are! (Photo: John Wadell)

Address: 120 N 10th St, Louisville, KY 40202
Website: kentuckypeerless.com

Kentucky Peerless didn't invent gift shop picks, they just perfected the concept. The idea of tasting through barrels, finding ones that have incredible taste profiles and then naming them and providing tasting notes is a real game-changer. It allows you to seek out what matches your personal flavor profile. They truly are unique and the fun comes in searching for those tasting notes as you try them.

Peerless is more than gift shop picks, though. They have an incredible story and very unique history you get to learn about on a tour. Of course the tour ends at a tasting bar where you can taste their product lineup and any featured gift shop picks.

I've got a lot of friends at Peerless, so be sure to say hello to John, Corky, Carson, Caleb, Alayna, Tommy, Nick, Cordell, Hunter and Rye the distillery cat for me while you are there!

Scorecard for This Assignment:
Score a KY Peerless Gift Shop Pick (1 Point): _____

Potential Bonus Points (Bonus Point(s) in Parenthesis):

Take a Tour (1 Point): _____

Say Hello to some of my Peerless Friends (1 Point): _____

TOTAL (3 Points Possible): _____

The Most Beautiful Distillery

Maker's Mark Distillery

The lake at Maker's Mark (Photo: Steve Akley)

Address: 3350 Burks Spring Rd, Loretto, KY 40037
Website: makersmark.com

There are a lot of reasons why Maker's Mark could be your favorite distillery tour. Maybe it's simply the beautiful grounds. It would be hard to argue there is a distillery with more scenic views. Then again, maybe it's cool history of the company you get educated on during the tour. Perhaps the art is the thing that keeps bringing you back. It could even be the food at the restaurant, or the great whisky or, well, you get it at this point. There is a lot to love about Maker's Mark.

Scorecard for This Assignment:
Tour Maker's Mark (1 Point): _____

Potential Bonus Points (Bonus Point(s) in Parenthesis):

Get a Hot Brown Star Hill Provisions (1 Point): _____

Get a Bourbon Slush at Star Hill's Bar (1 Point): _____

TOTAL (3 Points Possible): _____

Taste History

Justins' House of Bourbon

Address: 101 West Market Street, Louisville, KY 40202 or
601 W. Main Street, Lexington, KY 40508
Website: houseofbourbon.com

Owners Justin Sloan and Justin Thompson have a real winner
with their House of Bourbon concept. Yes, it's a regular liquor
store and yes, they have a tasting bar which is awesome.
They are also really making a name for themselves with store
picks, but, what really sets Justins' apart from everyone else is
the dusties.

Specializing in old bourbon, Justins' has set the standard of
what a Kentucky liquor store should be where you have the
friendly laws that allow them to buy vintage bourbon offerings.

Scorecard for This Assignment:
Visit Justins' House of Bourbon (1 Point): _____

Potential Bonus Points (Bonus Point(s) in Parenthesis):

Buy a barrel pick (1 Point): _____

Taste a dusty at the tasting bar (1 Point): _____

Buy a bottle released prior to 1990 (10 Points): _____

TOTAL (13 Points Possible): _____

Assignment #24   Bourbon Chocolates

A Place Where Chocolate is Art

Art Eatables

Chocolate Bourbon Truffles (Photo: Art Eatables)

Address: 819 West Main Street, Louisville, KY 40202 or 631 South 4th Street, Louisville, KY 40202 or 9816 Linn Station Road, Louisville, KY 40223
Website: arteatables.com

Kelly Ramsey, owner and "Cocktail Chocolatier" for Art Eatables is an amazing artist when it comes to the chocolate she creates. I'm talking from both the perspective of the look of her products (they are stunning) and, most importantly, the taste. Wowsers, she creates some amazing chocolates.

BOURBON ASSIGNMENTS | STEVE AKLEY, AUTHOR

Kelly isn't just a chocolate maker who has latched on to bourbon because it's trendy. She truly is part of the bourbon community. She is active at bourbon events. She posts frequently on a variety of bourbon topics in Facebook groups. It seems bourbon is as equal of a passion for her as chocolate.

This shows up in her stores. A visit to Art Eatables is like an express pass to the Kentucky Bourbon Trail because she works with so many distilleries to create unique treats featuring their bourbon. Seriously, you can get a truffle with Buffalo Trace, Jim Beam, Yellowstone, Willett, Wild Turkey and dozens more.

Scorecard for This Assignment:
Visit Art Eatables (1 Point): _____

Potential Bonus Points (Bonus Point(s) in Parenthesis):

Say hello to Kelly Ramsey (1 Point): _____

Buy some truffles (1 Point): _____

TOTAL (3 Points Possible): _____

"And they're off..."

Churchill Downs

You gotta see it in-person (Photo: Churchill Downs)

Address: 700 Central Ave, Louisville, KY 40208
Website: churchilldowns.com

You probably know Churchill Downs as the home of the world's most famous horse race, the Kentucky Derby. There is a lot more to Churchill Downs than a two-minute race held in May each year.

BOURBON ASSIGNMENTS | STEVE AKLEY, AUTHOR

While the Kentucky Derby is not my thing, it doesn't mean I don't love Churchill Downs. You can literally curate a day at Churchill Downs if you are willing to allocate that kind of time. We're talking tours, a museum, live events, food, a killer gift shop and, of course, horse racing.

Scorecard for This Assignment:
Visit Churchill Downs (1 Point): _____

Potential Bonus Points (Bonus Point(s) in Parenthesis):

Watch a horse race at Churchill Downs (1 Point): _____

Go on a tour of Churchill Downs (1 Point): _____

Tour the Kentucky Derby Museum (1 Point): _____

Get Your Photo with the Barbaro Statue in Front (1 Point): ___

Attend the Kentucky Derby (10 Points): _____

TOTAL (15 Points Possible): _____

5 Pointers

5

Assignment #26   Award Winning

Bottle Your Own Bourbon

Neeley Family Distillery

Neeley Family's Award Winning Bourbon (Photo: NFD)

Address: 4360 KY-1130, Sparta, KY 41086
Website: neeleyfamilydistillery.com

You could just go in and pick up a bottle of Neeley Family Distillery's award winning bourbon off the shelf, but why would you? You literally can shop like that anywhere. At Neeley, you can actually bottle, seal and label it your very own bottle so now you are talking a true bourbon experience. To top it off, all of Neeley's bourbon is single barrels so each one is unique and has its own character. Speaking of character, there are some real characters at Neeley Family Distillery. Pet Thumper the distillery cat (trust me, he'll be around), get PawPaw to acknowledge your existence (it was big for me when he started calling me by my last name, at least his version of it, "Egg-lee" but you gotta start with a hello) and get a photo with the beautiful, amazing, fun, Miss Beka Sue and pick up some bonus points!

Scorecard for This Assignment:
Fill Your Own Bottle at NFD (5 Points): _____

Potential Bonus Points (Bonus Point(s) in Parenthesis):

Pet Thumper (the distillery cat) (1 Point): _____

Get PawPaw to Acknowledge You (1 Point): _____

Get a Selfie with Miss Beka Sue (1 Point): _____

TOTAL (8 Points Possible): _____

Fried Chicken and Bourbon

The Purple Poulet

The Purple Poulet's Sign (Photo: Purple Poulet)

Address: 603 6th Avenue, Dayton, KY 41074
Website: purplepoulet.com

With places like New Riff, Neeley Family Distillery, Molly Wellmann's Japps Since 1879 and Revival Vintage Spirits in the Northern Kentucky/Cincinnati metro area, you end up needing a few cool places to eat. Purple Poulet is one of those little gems that you might not have heard about, but you have to stop and enjoy when you are out as a "bourbon person doing bourbon things." Their fried chicken is amazing and they've got a nice selection of bourbons including some vintage and tough to find offerings. Live like Colonel Steve at this one and order the chicken and waffle and you'll even pick up a bonus point!

Scorecard for This Assignment:

Eat at the Purple Poulet (5 Points): _____

Potential Bonus Points (Bonus Point(s) in Parenthesis):

Get the Fried Chicken and Waffle (1 Point): _____

Order a bourbon of your choice (1 Point): _____

TOTAL (7 Points Possible): _____

The Perfect Bourbon Mixer

Ale-8-One: A Kentucky Original

They just taste better in those returnable bottles
(Photo: Steve Akley)

Address: 25 Carol Rd, Winchester, KY 40391
Website: ale8one.com

Ale-8-One is an institution in Kentucky but largely unknown outside of the Bluegrass State. It's a shame because I love Ale-8 as it's commonly known and it mixes really well with bourbon if you are looking for a refreshing summer cocktail.

The regular is fantastic, the cherry they came out with a couple of years ago is also amazing and they have been doing special seasonal releases during the summer as well so it's a fun brand to keep up with.

The tours are free, but they are at specific times so you probably want to refer to the website prior to going (getting a reservation is also a good idea if you are going during the busy summer season). During the tour you see the entire process from company history, to formulation, bottling and quality control. The real highlight, though, is at the end, you get one of those old-school returnable glass bottle of Ale-8 served at the perfect temperature. The rumor is those returnable bottles make it taste better and while that sounds crazy, taste for yourself and you'll probably agree. I know I did!

Scorecard for This Assignment:
Take an Ale-8-One Tour (5 Points): _____

Potential Bonus Points (Bonus Point(s) in Parenthesis):

Taste a Cherry Ale-8 (1 Point): _____

Buy something Ale-8 branded in the gift shop (1 Point): _____

TOTAL (7 Points Possible): _____

Assignment #29   Dambo's Giants

Visit the Barrel People Family

Bernheim Arboretum and Research Forest

Little Elina (Photo: Steve Akley)

Address: 2075 Clermont Road, Clermont, KY 40110
Website: bernheim.org

Part of the celebration for the 90th anniversary of the Bernheim Arboretum and Research Forest was the installation of Denmark artist Thomas Dambo's giant trolls created from recycled bourbon barrels.

These huge sculptures range from 15 – 20 feet in height and make for a fun outing since it requires some hiking and navigation skills to find all three in the forest. Located right in the heart of Bourbon Country, this is a fun diversion from the distilleries, especially if you have children as the kids are allowed to touch and even climb on these statues.

Scorecard for This Assignment:
Visit Bernheim Forest (5 Points): _____

Potential Bonus Points (Bonus Points in Parenthesis):

Visit the Little Nis Sculpture (1 Point): _____

Visit the Mama Loumari Sculpture (1 Point): _____

Visit the Little Elina Sculpture (1 Point): _____

TOTAL (8 Points Possible): _____

Meet the People of Bourbon

The Kentucky Bourbon Festival

Jon the fun! (Photo: Kentucky Bourbon Festival)

Address: Bardstown, Kentucky
Website: kybourbonfestival.com

The Kentucky Bourbon Festival is the grand-daddy of bourbon festivals. Combine how long they've been doing this with the fact that the Festival itself is in the heart of Bourbon Country (Bardstown) and you've got one pretty cool event to attend. With a week of activities, there are plenty of great opportunities to meet bourbon celebrities and your fellow fans.

BOURBON ASSIGNMENTS | STEVE AKLEY, AUTHOR

Scorecard for This Assignment:

Attend the KY Bourbon Festival (5 Points): _____

Potential Bonus Points (Bonus Point(s) in Parenthesis):

Attend an educational session (1 Point): _____

Get a bottle signed (1 Point): _____

TOTAL (7 Points Possible): _____

Assignment #31   More Dusty Hunting

Why is the Old Stuff So Good?

Revival Vintage Spirits

Taste and buy! (Photo: Revival)

Address: 5 East 8th Street, Covington, KY 41011
Website: revivalky.com

Dusty Hunter Brad Bonds, along with his business partners
Shannon Smith and Katie Meyer have brought the concept of
a liquor store selling vintage bourbon to Northern Kentucky.
Vintage pours are affordably priced and the dusty selections
are great. Plus, the team keeps their website up-to-date so
you can map out a plan of what you want to taste and what
you want to buy before you even make the trek.

BOURBON ASSIGNMENTS | STEVE AKLEY, AUTHOR

Scorecard for This Assignment:

Visit Revival Vintage Spirits (5 Points):_____

Potential Bonus Points (Bonus Point(s) in Parenthesis):

Taste a dusty at the tasting bar (1 Point): _____

Buy a bottle released prior to 1990 (10 Points): _____

TOTAL (16 Points Possible): _____

The Start of the Bourbon Trail

Frazier Museum

The Bottle Hall (Photo: Frazier Museum)

Address: 829 W Main Street, Louisville, KY 40202
Website: fraziermuseum.org

You know you are in Kentucky when the local history museum has a big portion of its exhibit space dedicated to bourbon. This is the kind of culture I need in my life.

A few years ago the Frazier Museum partnered with the Kentucky Distillers Association (KDA) to expand its bourbon exhibits. They now call it the start of the Kentucky Bourbon Trail as it's home to so much history and brand information.

A few of the highlights include a bottle hall where you can see most of the bottles of Kentucky bourbon that are currently on the market and bourbon historian Chet Zoeller's vast collection of Pre-Prohibition bottles. I love seeing those old bottles and the artwork on them.

Of course every museum tour ends in a gift shop but this one is like no other because you can actually buy bourbon there.

Kentucky does it right!

<u>Scorecard for This Assignment:</u>
Visit the Frazier Museum (5 Points): _____

Potential Bonus Points (Bonus Point(s) in Parenthesis):

Find Neeley Family Distillery in the Bottle Hall (1 Point): _____

View Chet Zoeller's Bottle Collection (1 Point): _____

TOTAL (7 Points Possible): _____

Assignment #33   Visit a Castle!

Channel Colonel E.H. Taylor

Castle & Key Distillery

There's nothing like it! (Photo: Steve Akley)

Address: 4445 McCracken Pike, Frankfort, KY 40601
Website: castleandkey.com

Disney has its Magical Kingdom, but bourbon has Castle & Key. C&K truly is a magical place where you can't help but still feel the presence looming of Colonel Taylor. He was such a visionary to recognize the importance of building a place that not only welcomes visitors but is a monument to the quality he was putting inside of his bottles.

If this project was attempted today, I am sure it would be with cheap building materials and an outward facing façade that was meant to look like an old-time castle. This thing was really built with the quality of a medieval castle.

It's a powerful tour to go on as you factor in the history there and what has had to be done to rescue this incredible place from just crumbling away.

Your tour isn't complete, though, without a stroll through the grounds to see the perfectly manicured landscapes and botanical gardens.

Scorecard for This Assignment:
Visit Castle & Key (5 Points): _____

Potential Bonus Points (Bonus Point(s) in Parenthesis):

Take a Tour (1 Point): _____

Stroll the Beautiful Grounds (1 Point): _____

TOTAL (7 Points Possible): _____

A Free Attraction to Enjoy!

Oscar Getz Whiskey Museum

One of the displays (Photo: Oscar Getz Museum)

Address: Spalding Hall, 114 North Fifth Street, Bardstown, Kentucky 40004
Website: oscargetzwhiskeymuseum.com

Oscar Getz is a largely forgotten figure to today's bourbon consumers but he shouldn't be. Getz began his career in sales for a distributor but his success allowed him to work his way up to distillery owner as he bought the old Tom Moore Distillery. Under Getz's leadership, the company would change names to its current name, Barton and he was instrumental in developing many of the brands Barton 1792 sells today. He even expanded the business by buying out Glenmoor and was recognized as the bourbon industry's "Man of the Year" in both 1942 and 1957.

Throughout his career, Getz collected whiskey artifacts and memorabilia. He would display them at his Barton Distillery in Bardstown, Kentucky. Late in his career, as the collection outgrew the Visitor's Center at Barton, he looked for a permanent home. The city of Bardstown worked out a deal to take over the museum, finding it a home in an abandoned Catholic Seminary. Unfortunately, Getz would pass away in 1983 before the museum opened to the public.

Today, you can see the collection of historic artifacts spanning hundreds of years at the museum. Best of all, it's a free attraction.

Scorecard for This Assignment:
Tour Oscar Getz Museum (5 Points): _____

Potential Bonus Points (Bonus Point(s) in Parenthesis):

Make a donation to the Museum (1 Point): _____

TOTAL (6 Points Possible): _____

Sit Back and Relax

Limestone Branch Distillery

Hanging with the crew at Limestone (Photo: Justine Mays)

Address: 1280 Veterans Memorial Hwy, Lebanon, KY 40033
Website: limestonebranch.com

Distilleries are definitely something I enjoy but there are few I enjoy more than Limestone Branch. There's so much there. For starters, you can meet Steve Beam or Stephen Fante, or maybe even both. That right there is worth the trip.

But wait, there's more…

If that weren't enough, they have some of the best tours out there, particulary if you get Stephen Fante leading it. I love the fact you can get a cocktail or perhaps old Yellowstone release at the bar. You can sit back and look at the beautifully manicured grounds while enjoying that cocktail with a cigar on the porch. Let's not forget the gift shop! There is a lot of great logo merchandise as well as experiments you can only buy at the gift shop. Plus, if you happen to be there in the fall, you have to pick up the yearly Yellowstone L.E. release. It's one of my favorites each year and Steve Beam always does an amazing job of creating something very unique year-to-year.

With a possible 19 points to get… what are you waiting for? Get to Limestone Branch today!

Scorecard for This Assignment:
Visit Limestone Branch (5 Points): _____

Potential Bonus Points (Bonus Point(s) in Parenthesis):

Take a Tour (1 Point): _____

Get a Cocktail (1 Point): _____

Smoke a Cigar on the Porch (1 Point): _____

Buy one of the Experiments (1 Point): _____

Buy a 2021 Yellowstone L.E. in the Gift Shop (10 Points): ___

TOTAL (19 Points Possible): _____

Assignment #36   Visit A Wise Old Owl

Meet Dixon Dedman

Beaumont Inn

Beaumont's famous fried chicken (Photo: Beaumont Inn)

Address: 638 Beaumont Inn Drive, Harrodsburg, KY 40330
Website: beaumontinn.com

A proper visit to the Kentucky Bourbon Trail involves some "side-trip" adventures. You have to go beyond simply visiting distilleries, but it's also nice to not get too far out of the bourbon world when you are doing these things.

The Beaumont Inn is one of these perfect things to do as you further your Kentucky explorations. Not only is it a great meal, it's a fun old historical building to walk around. The food is all comfort foods, kind of like an old time family dinner when you dine there.

Of course, no trip to the Beaumont Inn is truly complete without a visit with the affable Dixon Dedman. He really is a joy to spend some time getting to know.

Definitely plan on having at least a lunch or dinner at the Beaumont Inn, but, if you can extend your time there, stop by their bar and even stay the night at the Inn. You won't be disappointed!

Scorecard for This Assignment:
Have a meal at the Beaumont Inn (5 Points): _____

Potential Bonus Points (Bonus Point(s) in Parenthesis):

Grab a drink at the Owl's Nest Bar (1 Point): _____

Spend the night at the Inn (10 Points): _____

TOTAL (16 Points Possible): _____

10 Pointers

10

Meet Molly Wellmann!

Japp's Since 1879

Molly and Me (Photo: Mandy Kaplan)

Address: 1134 Main St, Cincinnati, OH 45202
Website: jappsotr.com

During your bourbon travels, it's inevitable you will end up in Northern Kentucky. Taking a quick diversion across the river to go to Molly Wellmann's place is well worth your time. We're talking a cool atmosphere, great drinks and best of all, Molly herself.

Seriously, she's the most positive and cool person you will ever meet. She knows everything about cocktails, bourbon brands and bourbon history. A quick conversation with her will inspire you. One of the true bourbon bucketlist moments can happen here… we're talking about the World's Best Bartender (hey, she's won the award) making you the World's Best Old Fashioned (as voted by Steve Akley) is pretty special indeed!

BOURBON ASSIGNMENTS | STEVE AKLEY, AUTHOR

Scorecard for This Assignment:
Visit Japp's Since 1879 (10 Points): _____

Potential Bonus Points (Bonus Point(s) in Parenthesis):

Say Hello to Molly (1 Point): _____

Order an Old Fashioned (1 Point): _____

TOTAL (12 Points Possible): _____

Assignment #38   The Ultimate Tour

A Freddie Johnson Tour

Buffalo Trace Distillery

Freddie Johnson (Photo: Buffalo Trace)

Address: 113 Great Buffalo Trace, Frankfort, KY 40601
Website: buffalotracedistillery.com

A Freddie Johnson tour is like nothing else in bourbon. It's an education about process, brand and family history. Freddie will wow you with knowledge, he'll make you laugh with his jokes and funny sayings ("Isn't that cool?") and be prepared as you might even get a little teary-eyed when he shares some personal stories. The only problem is the fact there is no clear path to book a "Freddie tour." Tours aren't assigned to tour guides in advance so when you book you don't know who will

BOURBON ASSIGNMENTS | STEVE AKLEY, AUTHOR

be leading yours. Basically, you just have to book and hope for the best. The tours normally fill up so you do have to book in advance with the exception of the slower winter months so you could possibly show up in January or February during the week and ask if Freddie is giving tours and if he has any openings but beyond that you will need to have luck on your side!

Scorecard for This Assignment:
Go on a Freddie led tour (10 Points): _____

Potential Bonus Points (Bonus Point(s) in Parenthesis):

Ask a question on the tour (1 Point): _____

TOTAL (11 Points Possible): _____

Assignment #39   Distillers Summit

Our Yearly Trip to Key West

January 27 – 30, 2022

The Crew at Hemmingway's House (Photo: Steve Akley)

Address: Key West Florida
Website: abvnetwork.com/distillers-summit

Key West is the ultimate adult playground. The weather is good all year round, the bars are stellar and there is a lot of tourist activities to customize your trip. That's why we established the Distillers Summit in 2020, an industry getaway to paradise in what has to be the worst time of the year for weather around the country. In Key West, it's shorts and Tommy Bahama shirts all the time!

A couple of my favorites are there. I love visting the Hemmingway House when I'm there. I love the history, the

Hemmingway stories and all of those cats. Sloppy Joe's is one of my all-time favorite bars. We're talking live entertainment, good food and plenty of rum cocktails.

So join us for some bourbon business meetings, some beautiful sunsets and plenty of laughs with friends.

Scorecard for This Assignment:
Join us in Key West (10 Points): _____

Potential Bonus Points (Bonus Point(s) in Parenthesis):

Stay Up Past 2:00 AM at Least Once (1 Point): _____

Wear a Tommy Bahama Shirt (1 Point): _____

Drink at Sloppy Joe's (1 Point): _____

Tour Hemmingway's House (1 Point): _____

TOTAL (14 Points Possible): _____

Assignment #40   BBQ Pork Chop

The Ultimate Bucket List Item

Barbecue at Fred Noe's House

Just add Booker's (Photo: Can Stock Photo/2002Lubava1981)

Address: Bardstown, Kentucky
Website: jimbeam.com

When I started my personal bourbon journey, I made a list of things I wanted to do in bourbon. This was a combination of personal and professional goals that would ensure I was contributing to the industry and having fun as well. Through the years, it's been fun to check off just about everything on that list. One item remains elusive, though… the barbecue at Fred Noe's house.

Wait, could that be a thing? Something you put on a bourbon assignments list? Absolutely! It represents the ultimate bourbon experience.

Think about it… Fred Noe and his son Freddie live next door to one another. We're talking about descendants of the Beam family the greatest name in bourbon. They live in the house Jim Beam himself once lived in. Cooking was one of Booker

Noe's favorite hobbies. Today, Fred Noe is known for his great barbecuing skills. I've spoken to all kinds of Beam sales reps and dignitaries… people who have scored that exclusive invite to the Noe's home for a Fred Noe barebecue and they all talk about how great of an experience it is. The history that's there and those huge pork chops finished in a blaze of glory as Fred sears them with a huge flame created when he dumps Booker's across that open flame.

Damn, I can almost taste it now as I write about it. Still, it eludes me and I'm not sure how you get the invite. That's the cool thing about bourbon. You don't know when you are going to score that really tough-to-find bottle. You don't know when someone is going to randomly ask you to join their barrel pick and yes, you don't know when you will get the invite to experience that backyard pork chop, but somehow, some way if you keep thinking it will happen, it just might.

Just remember, you have to be invited for this one… you can't just show up!

Scorecard for This Assignment:
Get Invited to a Fred Noe BBQ (10 Points): _____

Potential Bonus Points (Bonus Point(s) in Parenthesis):

Don't Make a Fool of Yourself (1 Point): _____

TOTAL (11 Points Possible): _____

Grand Total Worksheet

Use this worksheet to calculate all of the activity you completed between the time you bought the book and December 31, 2022. If you would like to submit your total for consideration to come onto an episode of The Bourbon Daily to discuss your bourbon adventures while completing your bourbon assignments, send photos of your worksheet to Steve Akley: *abvsales@abvnetwork.com*.

#1/Michters (2 Points Possible): _____

#2/Bourbon Barrel Foods (2 Points Possible): _____

#3/Merle's (2 Points Possible): _____

#4/OldFo Water Tower (2 Points Possible): _____

#5/Jim Beam (4 Points Possible): _____

#6/Fante's Coffee Shop (2 Points Possible): _____

#7/The Old Seelbach Bar (3 Points Possible): _____

#8/Lousivlle Visitor's Center (3 Points Possible): _____

#9/Handy Food Mart (4 Points Possible): _____

#10/Toddy's Liquors (2 Points Possible): _____

#11/Heaven Hill (3 Points Possible): _____

#12/Proof on Main (4 Points Possible): _____

#13/James E. Pepper (3 Points Possible): _____

BOURBON ASSIGNMENTS | STEVE AKLEY, AUTHOR

#14/Crank and Boom (2 Points Possible): _____

#15/Westport Whiskey and Wine (3 Points Possible): _____

#16/Whiskey Dry (4 Points Possible): _____

#17/Old Forester (2 Points Possible): _____

#18/Bourbons Bistro (7 Points Possible): _____

#19/Jeff Ruby's (5 Points Possible): _____

#20/Virtual Bourbon (2 Points Possible): _____

#21/KY Peerless (3 Points Possible): _____

#22/Maker's Mark (3 Points Possible): _____

#23/Justins' House of Bourbon (13 Points Possible): _____

#24/Art Eatables (3 Points Possible): _____

#25/Churchill Downs (15 Points Possible): _____

#26/Neeley Family Distillery (8 Points Possible): _____

#27/Purple Poulet (7 Points Possible): _____

#28/Ale-8-One (7 Points Possible): _____

#29/Bernheim Forest (8 Points Possible): _____

#30/KY Bourbon Festival (7 Points Possible): _____

#31/Revival Vintage Spirits (16 Points Possible): _____

BOURBON ASSIGNMENTS | STEVE AKLEY, AUTHOR

#32/Frazier Museum (7 Points Possible): _____

#33/Castle and Key (7 Points Possible): _____

#34/Oscar Getz Museum (6 Points Possible): _____

#35/Limestone Branch (19 Points Possible): _____

#36/Beaumont Inn (16 Points Possible): _____

#37/Japp's Since 1879 (12 Points Possible): _____

#38/Freddie Johnson Tour (11 Points Possible): _____

#39/Key West (14 Points Possible): _____

#40/Barbecue at the Noe's (11 Points Possible): _____

Bonus Points:

Author Autograph (10 Points): _____

Foreword Author Autograph (10 Points): _____

Autographs* (35 Points Possible): _____

*See bonus autographs section on page 101.

309 Possible Points

How did you do? Good luck and happy bourbon adventures!

About the Author

Steve Akley is a Kentucky Colonel, author, podcaster, movie producer, eMagazine publisher, web series talk show host, and most of all: a bourbon fan. This St. Louis resident enjoys spending his spare time learning about and discussing all-things bourbon. Follow his journey under the name @steveakley on all social media or via his website: abvnetwork.com.

Special Thanks

Much Appreciation for Those That Helped

My wife, "The Warden" for her help in editing this book.

My buddy, Mark Hansen, for the great cover design.

All of the great businesses that helped inspire the book.

All of my friends in Kentucky who make me feel at home every time I visit.

You, the reader. Your support is what allows me to live my dream of doing what I am doing in the bourbon industry.

Bonus Points – Autographs

Autographs are a great way to connect with the people of bourbon. Whether it's a well-known person like Kentucky Bourbon Hall-of-Famer Eddie Russell, or perhaps just the person who took you on a tour at your favorite distillery. They are all worth talking to and interacting with. While you are at it, have them autograph your book. You'll get 1 bonus point each for the first 10 you get and you can get up to 25 additional points for collecting 5 Kentucky Bourbon Hall-of-Famers (5 points each). That's the potential for 35 extra points, all for starting up conversations with people you probably want to talk to anyway.

<u>**Scorecard for This Assignment:**</u>
Autographs of People in the Bourbon Biz (1 point each with a maximum of 10 total points):_____

Potential Bonus Points (Bonus Point(s) in Parenthesis):

Kentucky Bourbon Hall-of-Famer* Autographs (5 points each with a maximum total of 25 points): _____

TOTAL (35 Points Possible): _____

Autographs

Autographs

Autographs

Autographs

THE END

Made in the USA
Monee, IL
04 November 2021